Seasoned with Salt

*how the art of public speaking can
sharpen your message and extend your reach*

Ryan Cummings

Guy E. Warner

Seasoned with Salt
© 2019 by DeWard Publishing Company, Ltd.
P.O. Box 290696, Tampa, FL 33687
www.deward.com

All rights reserved. No portion of this book may be reproduced in any form without written permission from the publisher.

Cover by nvoke design.

All Bible quotations are taken from the The Holy Bible, English Standard Version®, copyright © 2001 by Crossway Bibles, a publishing ministry of Good News Publishers. Used by permission. All rights reserved. Any emphasis in Bible quotations is added.

Reasonable care has been taken to trace original sources for any excerpts and quotations appearing in this book and to document such information. For material not in the public domain, fair use standards and practices were followed. Should any attribution be found to be incorrect or incomplete, the publisher welcomes written documentation supporting correction for subsequent printing.

Printed in the United States of America.

ISBN: 978-1-947929-06-7

Contents

SECTION 1 – Introduction
1. Introduction and Overview of COD 7
2. The Joy of Preaching. 11

SECTION 2 – Content
3. The Character of the Speaker 17
4. The Listening Process 23
5. Audience Analysis. 29
6. Finding a Topic 35
7. Gathering Materials. 41

SECTION 3 – Organization
8. Organization. .49
9. Organizational Patterns 55
10. Introductions and Conclusions. 61

SECTION 4– Delivery
11. Controlling Fear 69
12. Verbal Delivery and Language 75
13. Nonverbal Delivery. 81

14. Vocal Delivery .85

15. PowerPoint Etiquette 89

SECTION 5 – Conclusion
16. Conclusion 97

APPENDICES
Appendix A: Audience Analysis Form. 101

Appendix B: Sample Sermon Outline 103

Appendix C: Speaking Evaluation Form. 107

Appendix D: PSA Form. 109

Appendix E: Recommended Resources 111

Notes. 113

SECTION ONE

Introduction

1

COD

The Basics of Speech

Becoming a skilled speaker is no different from learning any new skill: One must master the basics before advancing to competency. In basketball, for example, one must learn to guard, dribble, and shoot before becoming a skilled player. In speech, you can learn the basic components of speaking skills by using the acronym COD; this acronym derives from the second author's lifelong nickname, Doc. Moreover, effective speech involves *Content, Organization, and Delivery*.

Competent speech truly is more than just fashionable eloquence; it involves COD, especially in the realm of Biblical talks. The objective of all Bible talks and sermons should be to "preach the good news" (Rom 10.15) of Jesus by being God's messengers.[1] Indeed, our goal is to proclaim the message of Jesus as clearly as possible, so that our audience may understand. Doing so requires consideration of *what* is said (Content) and *how* it's said (Organization and Delivery). While future chapters will investigate each of these domains more thoroughly, the sections below will introduce the main tenets of COD.

Content

Content should be the starting place for any speaker. Too often speakers worry about how they will be heard without worrying enough about what they will say. Furthermore, becoming skilled in delivery is often easier than becoming skilled in selecting and writing content. Competency in content requires work and dedication. Messengers of the Gospel message should make two main considerations for Content: (1) What does God want me to say, based on His Word? and (2) What does my audience need to hear?

Much like Paul, we are "instruments" (Acts 9.15) of God. As such, our mission as speakers should be to speak the message of God. Thus, the first step in becoming a skilled speaker is to learn and understand the message of the Bible. We must be "devoted" to the reading of Scripture and the study of the Word of God (1 Tim 4.13). Likewise, as God "has spoken to us by His Son" (Heb 1.2), we must know Jesus and emulate His qualities in our lives before taking His message to the pulpit. Indeed, any messenger of the Gospel message must be godly, devoted to the Scripture and the path of godliness.

While the importance of godliness to effective speaking cannot be overemphasized, a competent speaker cannot underestimate the importance of audience analysis. When choosing a topic, a speaker must consider not what he wants to say but what his audience needs to hear. Following the example of Paul, we should speak "all for your upbuilding, beloved" (2 Cor 12.19). What are the issues or challenges that our audience is facing, to which the Word of God can provide a solution? Upon choosing a topic, the competent speaker must ensure he feeds his audience a healthy diet, teaching "what accords with sound doctrine" (Tit 2.1). In summary, content should start with a godly life motivated by the Word of God and end with the edification of our audience.

Organization

After considering content, speakers should consider how best to organize a talk. This is, in our opinion, the most missed aspect of speaking by messengers of the Gospel. Speakers should give careful attention not only to what they want to say but also how they want to say it and in what order they want to say it. Effective organization should present a talk in a way in which the speaker can remember the message and in which the audience can understand. In a later chapter, we will provide different strategies for organization (e.g., topical, problem-solution, cause-effect, etc.), but the central consideration should be to organize your message in a way that is clear and effective.

Delivery

While organization ensures the content is clear in preparation, delivery ensures the content is clear in presentation. Moreover, delivery concerns the nonverbal aspects of communication such as rate, tone, gestures, posture, eye contact, etc. Our goal with delivery is not to impress but to communicate a clear message. Indeed, Paul said that he came not "with lofty speech or wisdom" (1 Cor 2.1), that is smooth words simply designed to impress an audience. Rather, the focus of Paul's message was "not ourselves, but Jesus Christ as Lord" (2 Cor 4.5). Skilled speakers should aim for clarity and must practice before speaking; more specific recommendations and practical exercises will be offered in a later chapter. Again, the focus should be on the content of the message, considering how best to present it through delivery.

2

THE JOY OF PREACHING

Why Preach?

Before explaining how to prepare and present an effective Bible talk, we need to examine why we should preach. While brethren may joke about the easy life of a preacher, there are few activities as spiritually demanding and emotionally challenging as preaching. Thus, a preacher needs a proper motivation in his work. Furthermore, some preachers are motivated by wrong motives, such as "selfish ambition" (Phil 1.17), and need to either correct their attitude or cease the work.

Preachers should preach not out of zeal for self-exaltation but out of service to Christ. The books of 2 Corinthians, 1 Timothy, 2 Timothy, and Titus explain the basics of preaching as clearly as any books in the New Testament. Paul summarizes the proper motivation for preaching by telling Timothy, "If you put these things before the brothers, you will be a good servant of Christ Jesus..." (1 Tim 4.6). Indeed, we should preach because we desire to serve Christ Jesus!

Only a commitment to Christ can motivate a preacher to preach effectively. While self-motivated preachers seek compliments, servants of Christ recognize our outcome is far more important. Paul proceeded to tell Timothy, "Persist in this, for by so doing you will save both yourself and your hearers" (1 Tim 4.16). Ultimately, Paul urges us to recognize that salvation of our hearers' souls is at stake, and a true commitment to Christ will motivate us to work toward this end.

The Discouragement of Preachers

To those who preach, or have preached, this chapter title ("The Joy of Preaching") may seem ironic and even confusing. Too often messengers of God's Word become discouraged, some even to the point of giving up, because of their honest efforts to lead men and women to the gospel. We know of men who have abandoned the pulpit for secular jobs because of the pushback from angry, disgruntled brethren. Many preachers expect loving acceptance of the Word from brethren, only to be met with apathetic or angry facial expressions while preaching; some brethren go even further by leaving the building or insulting the message.

Preachers throughout Biblical history faced pushback and even persecution because of their words. We have been preceded by such notable servants as Moses and a succession of bold prophets, some of whom faced deprivation and death sentences for the privilege of being God's mouthpieces. The apostles left us a permanent and infallible record of how the Lord Himself suffered at the hands of Jewish authorities, the common people, masses of His followers, and even His earthly family. It came down to their misunderstanding and outright hatred of His preaching. We know there are times we can expect no less. After all, as Jesus said, "A servant is not greater than his master. If they persecuted Me, they will also persecute you" (John 15.20). Later by inspiration Paul echoed Christ's words when he wrote: "…we preach Christ crucified, a stumbling block to the Jews and folly to the Gentiles" (1 Cor 1.23).

Finding Joy in the Midst of Discouragement

Discouragement and negative reception is inevitable for every preacher, so what is the source of joy in communicating God's Word in talks and sermons? For Paul, his source of joy was not the external outcomes of his preaching but the internal changes of his hearers. He was no stranger to persecution but persisted in his work "to advance the gospel" (Phil 1.12). Regardless of the opposition he met most everywhere he preached, Paul felt joy when honest hearts responded to the gospel. Paul lived out the message he offered to Timothy, finding joy in his service to Christ by advancing the gospel in the lives of his hearers.

Like Paul, you too will sometimes face resistance to your efforts. However, like that grand apostle, you will also find joy in preparing and presenting His Word. Learn to temporarily ignore, and even pity, those who resist the holy message. There may be an occasion to speak privately with a brother or sister who opposes you and/or the gospel, but don't give up public preaching. As all who preached in the first century, you either plant the seed, water it, or both (1 Cor 3.5–9). Ask God for strength to speak again and again. Though we are nothing and God is everything, spreading the Word is both our duty and our blessing. Whether few or many "come forward," keep on preaching. Rarely do we know what occurs in the minds of listeners, but the gospel is "the power of God for salvation to everyone who believes…" (Rom 1.16). It will bear fruit because of or in spite of our efforts. You are privileged to speak not only truth, but *the* truth. Your joy will be fulfilled, if not in this life, then in the one to come.

SECTION TWO

Content

3

THE CHARACTER OF THE SPEAKER

Good content is contingent on good character. Thus, before explaining the factors of effective speaking in subsequent chapters, we would like to emphasize the importance of godly character in this chapter. Anyone can learn to use proper gestures while speaking or to develop a strong speaking voice, but great sermons can only come from godly speakers. For this reason, Paul admonished Timothy, "Keep a close watch on yourself and on the teaching" (1 Tim 4.16).

Characteristics of Good Character

No two books of the Bible better describe the ideal character of a speaker than First and Second Timothy. In his first letter to this young evangelist, Paul identified two critical aspects of character: faith and a good conscience (1 Tim 1.19). Both of these qualities (i.e., faith and a good conscience) should define the lives of godly speakers, shaping both their actions and their sermons. Without these, Paul warned, our faith can "make shipwreck" (1 Tim 1.19). We know too many brethren, especially preachers, who have lost their faith and thus their influence for Christ. To avoid such pitfalls and to stay effective in the kingdom, preachers need faith and a good conscience.

Faith

What quality defined God's messengers throughout Scripture? Why did God choose men like Moses, Samuel, Elijah, Isaiah, Peter, Stephen, and Paul to be His spokesmen? Faith! In spite of their weaknesses, these men had faith in God and His promises, so they served as capable presenters of His message. As Hebrews 11 so clearly demonstrates, every Christian—but especially preachers—need a strong faith in God to glorify Him, for "without faith it is impossible to please Him" (Heb 11.6). Yes, our faith can—and must—increase throughout our lives (Luke 17.5), but faith in God is a necessary prerequisite of speaking His Word.

Just as faith should lead to godly works in every Christian's life (Jas 2.14), the speaker's conduct should evidence a true faith. Paul admonished Timothy to be an example to fellow believers "in speech, in conduct, in love, in faith, in purity" (1 Tim 4.12). Indeed, our works and our words should follow from a sincere faith. In reference to our actions, we should practice what we preach. For example, Paul explained that "the Lord's servant must not be quarrelsome but kind to everyone" (2 Tim 2.24). As speakers and preachers, we must have faith in God and His commands, thus being kind to all. As another example, preachers must put faith in God, not money, staying clear of greed and its consequences (1 Tim 6.10).

Indeed, our actions should follow the teachings of the gospel, living the Faith that we proclaim.

Likewise, our words reveal much about our character, whether faithful or faithless to God. Our teaching should "agree with the sound words of our Lord Jesus Christ" (1 Tim 6.3). When God's Word is part of our daily speech, there is little to criticize. Furthermore, our daily language should "always be gracious, seasoned with salt" so that we "may know how" we "ought to answer each person" (Col 4.6). Words do matter. We need to avoid "foolish, ignorant controversies" (2 Tim 2.23) and have no part with "filthiness nor foolish talk nor crude joking" (Eph 5.4). Such are "not fitting" for a Christian. Solomon advises that "a word fitly spoken is like apples of gold in a setting of silver" (Prov 25.11). Words not fitly spoken, then, can have the converse effect. They can draw an audience closer, or drive them away; they can persuade or dissuade. Our words, whether chosen carefully or carelessly, can have a lasting impact (Jas 3). They should be chosen prayerfully. Therefore, good speakers live with faith, as is evidenced in their works and their words.

Good Conscience

Good character also speaks to Paul's second characteristic of a good preacher, that of maintaining a good conscience. Earlier in 1 Timothy 1, Paul instructed the young evangelist to command some Ephesian brethren to love "from a pure heart and a good conscience and a sincere faith" (1.5). Thus, faith and a good conscience are obviously intertwined; they speak of personal honesty. Lacking faith should automatically result in a defective conscience while a true faith will result in a clean conscience. Our lives should accord with the standard that we teach; failing to do so will strike our consciences. Stated another way, we should avoid hypocrisy, living a sincere life that comes from a sincere faith.

For men in particular, purity often provides one of the greatest barriers to a good conscience. Too often preachers proclaim the dangers of the works of the flesh while secretly giving into their own carnal passions. To fulfill Paul's command, we must live pure lives. Ultimately, purity concerns holiness, which refers to the process of being separated unto God. When we remember God and His character, His holiness should drive impurity from our lives. While holiness itself is a lifelong process, we should never cease our quest to be like God. Yes, we will never achieve perfection in this life, but, like Paul, we should "press on to make it our own" (Phil 3.12). When we sin, we should confess our sin, and Jesus will "cleanse us from all unrighteousness" (1 John 1.9). Only as we seek holiness and put off sin can we live with a good conscience before our glorious God.

The Consequences of Character

Good character is mandatory. It will either contribute to or detract from one's message. We will craft good content only when we have faith and a good conscience. As our understanding of God and our lives of obedience to Him improve, so will the depth and impact of our messages. Quintilian, an ancient Roman rhetorician, defined rhetoric as "a good man speaking well,"[2] and such a recognition has no greater importance than when preaching the gospel.

It has been said, especially in sermons, that "reputation is what men think we are, and character is what God knows we are."[3] There is no doubt the all-knowing God sees deeply into human souls and perfectly knows character. However, others will judge our character based on our works and words, and our reputation will soon follow. Communication scholars refer to this reputation--or perceived character--as ethos. Our message will have impact only so far as our audience perceives us as credible and trustworthy. Thus, we must avoid any actions that harm our ethos. Especially in the digital age, we must ensure that our online presence is holy and free from immorality. Only then will our words have impact. Truly, good speaking begins with good character.[4]

4

THE LISTENING PROCESS

Before detailing the specifics of effective speeches in the following chapters, we would like to provide a macro view of the communication process. By its nature, face-to-face communication is interactional, meaning that at least two people send messages back and forth, affecting each other through feedback. Even when you speak, you are sending verbal messages to your audience, and your audience is sending you nonverbal feedback. As a speaker, your goal is to maximize your audience's understanding of your messages. Learning to do so effectively requires an examination of the listening process.

Hearing vs. Listening

Within the context of a public speech, the main objective of the audience is to receive the message, yet not everyone does so to the same level of competence. The truth is, listening is complex, and people often do it poorly. In the process of receiving messages, we must differentiate between two terms: hearing and listening. Strictly speaking, **hearing** is the physiological process of receiving sounds. Of course, some people can hear better than others; age and environmental factors (e.g., loud noises or inadequate sound systems) often play a determining factor in one's ability to hear. On the other hand, **listening** is the psychological process of receiving another's message. Thus, audiences can hear a speaker's sounds without truly listening to his message. Jesus acknowledged those who heard but did not listen when He stated, "You will indeed hear but never understand" (Matt 13.14). Many heard the words of Jesus, but only some understood what He was saying.

The Goals of Listening

Successful listening, as opposed to mindless hearing, depends as much on the speaker as on the audience; together, the speaker and audience must accomplish the three key goals of listening: attention, comprehension, and retention.[5] First, to achieve listening from the audience, a speaker must gain an audience's **attention**, which is the focusing on a single stimulus to the exclusion of others. Practically, you are seeking for the audience to focus on your message as opposed to distractions, whether physical disruptions from the room such as crying children or mental disruptions from their own thoughts such as what they may have for lunch. Within a speech, introductions serve a critical role in gaining an audience's attention.

After gaining an audience's attention, a skilled speaker should seek an audience's **comprehension**. Comprehension takes an audience from hearing words to understanding the speaker's message. Listening demands a receiver's interpretation of the sender's message, so in many ways, comprehension is the most difficult of the goals of listening for the speaker to accomplish. Comprehension depends on a listener's physiological and psychological state, so the level of comprehension will depend on the individual listener. The selection of your topic, the thoughts you present, the organization of your speech, and your delivery all contribute to an audience's comprehension of the message.

Third, effective listening requires audiences to remember the message after the speech is complete, encompassing the goal of **retention**. Of the three goals of listening, this one is perhaps most difficult for a speaker to enact within his audience. Repetition is necessary for retention. A speaker may repeat key points throughout the message, which may increase the audience's retention, but audience members must often consider the information after the sermon to fully retain the message. Repetition, powerful persuasive appeals, clear illustrations, strong conclusions, and effective organizational patterns can all contribute to an audience's retention of the message.

A fourth goal of listening, unique to persuasive communication, is **acceptance**. As we will explain in the next chapter more fully, speakers often seek to change the beliefs, attitudes, and even values of their audience. Successful persuasion yields an audience's acceptance of the speaker's message. We will address the persuasive process more fully in Chapter 7, but skilled speakers know how to craft messages their audiences will accept. Conducting audience analysis, knowing an audience's values, making persuasive appeals, and warranting your claims can all aid an audience's acceptance of a persuasive message.

Motivations for Listening

In addition to the goals of effective listening, there are also various motivations for listening; Communication scholars have identified four relevant to preaching: to obtain information, to understand, to learn, and to be entertained.[6] While preachers often assume their audiences' presence demonstrates their desire to listen to the message, this is often not the case. Thus, preachers must learn to engage their audiences by seizing upon one of the general motivations for listening.

Moreover, preachers can capture an audience's attention by utilizing the various motivations for listening. To some degree, these motivations for listening resemble different types of media and various genres of literature. We may read the newspaper to obtain information, watch an instructional video to gain understanding, listen to a Ted Talk to learn, or listen to the radio for enjoyment. In reference to obtaining information, a speaker can present new information from the Bible to gain the audience's attention. The sixty-six books of the Bible contain so much interesting information that we can always find nuggets that even mature Christians may not know. To capture the attention of an audience, we may explain a concept that they have not understood before. Audiences frequently lack understanding of such important topics as God's grace or inerrancy of Scripture, so we can grab their attention by increasing their understanding. We can likewise capture their attention by recognizing an audience's desire to learn. While enjoyment may seem out of place in sermons, we can help audiences see the beauty and splendor of God's Word, increasing their personal enjoyment of listening to its teachings.

Barriers to Listening

It does not require much self-reflection to realize that listening can be difficult. How often do our minds wander from the message as we listen to a sermon? To maintain our audience's attention, we must be mindful of the various barriers to listening. The most pervasive barrier is our limited **attention span**, the ability to focus on one stimulus at a given time.[7] Listening can be compared to a revolving door. We attend to a message for a moment, change our focus to another thought, then take a tangential path to another thought, then become distracted by another thought, etc. Thoughts are constantly passing in and out of our minds. Thus, a skilled speaker must adapt to the attention span of his audience, keeping their attention on the message in spite of distractions. We will offer further recommendations for maintaining your audience's attention in future chapters.

Furthermore, as Jesus recognized in Matthew 13.10–17, the heart can provide a barrier to listening. We can speak with the eloquence of Aristotle and the zeal of Paul, but our words may fall upon deaf ears. No communication theory or psychological construct can overcome a closed heart. However, just as God told Ezekiel, our audience's failure to listen does not negate our command to preach His Word (Ezek 2.5). May we seek the listening of our audiences, and may God bless them with open ears to listen to His Word.

Finally, personal factors may affect your audience's ability to listen. Our individual experiences act as filters through which we interpret meaning. No two people share the same experiences, so no two people listen to messages and interpret their meanings in the exact same manner. Age, education, IQ, personal listening acuity, personal upbringing, and even gender may affect your audience's listening. Skilled speakers must consider how their audiences will listen to their messages. We will address this process more in the following chapter.

5

Audience Analysis

When preparing a speech, the topic and content should be audience-centered, rather than speaker-centered. The skilled speaker should analyze who the audience is, what they believe, and how best to communicate the content so that the audience can understand. Indeed, a sermon that may be effective for one audience may be ineffective for another; the skilled speaker must analyze to know the difference. This rule of audience-centered (or person-centered) communication is true of all communication episodes, with skilled speakers strategically crafting messages for their receivers.[8] This chapter explains how to choose a topic in light of audience analysis. See Appendix A for an audience analysis form.

The Elements of Audience Analysis

While it may be impossible for a speaker to know everything about his audience, asking certain questions can assist him in choosing a relevant topic and constructing an effective talk. Doing such requires the speaker to take the perspective of the audience. Far too often, speakers skip this critical step, rather considering only their own perspective and beliefs. Rather, we are to consider our audience "so that you may know how you ought to answer each person" (Col. 4.6). In general, the skilled speaker should ask who the listeners are (demographics) and what they believe (psychographics).[9]

Demographics

Demographics refer to the physical, racial, and sociological composition of the listeners. Analyzing demographics should aid the speaker in identifying the questions, the spiritual needs, and the problems that the audience members have. While choosing a topic can be a daunting task, demographics can lead a speaker to choosing a relevant topic for the audience. By completing such an analysis, a speaker can choose a relevant topic for audiences, both ones they know well and even ones they have never met.

There are various demographics a speaker should consider. Such characteristics include the age, the size, the gender, the education, the professions, the perceived spiritual maturity, the perceived level of Bible knowledge, and the family structures of the audience. While considering all of these characteristics may give the speaker a general idea of the audience, certain characteristics can lead to specific topics. For example, if a congregation consists mainly of older women, a sermon on training the younger women from Titus 2 may be more relevant than a sermon on parenting from Ephesians 5. Likewise, if an audience consists mainly of recent converts, a sermon on the first principles in Hebrews 5 may be more effective than a sermon comparing the various sacrifices in Leviticus; such a sermon on the sacrifices would be more effective for an audience with more Bible knowledge. Indeed, such analysis should lead to effective preaching.

Beyond considering demographic factors, a skilled speaker should also consider how similar (homogenous) or different (heterogenous) an audience is. The more the audience has in common, the easier selecting a topic should be as members of a common demographic group often have similar concerns, beliefs, and spiritual needs. The beliefs and needs of a seventy-year-old, for example, are often different from those of a seventeen-year-old. As the typical morning and evening audiences represent a cross section of ages, genders, educational levels, professions, and experiences, a speaker must determine which group to focus on (i.e., the target audience). For example, if an audience is heterogeneous with different ages and levels of spiritual maturity, your target audience on Sunday may be those not yet in Christ, preaching on the blessings in Christ in Ephesians 1, while another week your target audience may be older Christians facing discouragement, preaching on encouragement from 1 Peter 1. A skilled speaker will know whom he is addressing and focus on all different groups of an audience over time.

Psychographics

After choosing a topic based on an audience's demographics, a speaker must consider how to address it by analyzing an audience's psychographics, which are the beliefs, attitudes, and values of a prospective audience.[10] Indeed, a speaker should seek to present with the consideration of the audience's psychographics in mind, rather than his own.[11] As audiences may hold views far different from the speaker, considering psychographics accords with Christ's command to the apostles, "'Behold, I am sending you out as sheep in the midst of wolves, so be wise as serpents and innocent as doves" (Matt 10.16). Not considering psychographics can make or break an otherwise well-intended effort.

Beliefs, attitudes, and values all relate to one another and make up an individual's disposition toward a topic. A belief is an individual's conviction that something is true; an attitude is an individual's emotional or moral evaluation of a belief; and a value is the worth that individuals assign to beliefs. To illustrate, an individual may believe that the Bible is not inspired; hold the attitude that the Bible is unimportant to life; and value freedom from morality over truth. A sermon about inspiration from 2 Timothy 3.16–17 to that individual would be received far differently from someone who believes that the Bible is inspired, holds the attitude that the Bible is important to life, and values truth over freedom from morality. The skilled speaker must be aware of such differences and consider how to overcome them in the presentation.

As values are most deep-seated, they are most difficult to change. Moreover, values influence attitudes, which influence beliefs. Effective preaching must address the disparate values or attitudes to change beliefs. Consider, for example, a sermon on the Christian and politics. Such a sermon must operate not at the level of beliefs but at the level of values. Usually, those in favor of more political involvement value a Christian's influence in all aspects of the world while those in favor of less political involvement value God's providence in all aspects of the world. If a sermon seeks to change an audience's beliefs on the issue without addressing the disparate values, such a sermon will be ineffective. A speaker must be especially aware of values when dealing with controversial topics. An effective sermon on gay marriage must deal with sanctity of marriage versus perceived equality. An effective sermon on abortion must deal with sanctity of life versus perceived choice. Indeed, values drive beliefs yet are the most difficult to change. In summary, analyzing psychographics assists in understanding how an audience will receive a topic and how a speaker should approach it.

Social judgment theory, a social psychology theory, may help you analyze your audience's values.[12] The theory claims that we have three "latitudes" for receiving information: rejection, acceptance, and noncommitment. Each of these latitudes is intensified by one's involvement (i.e., the felt personal importance) with the issue. For example, nearly everyone has a high level involvement for abortion. If you preach that "abortion is sinful," this message will fall on the extreme ends of one's latitude of rejection or latitude of acceptance. However, if you preach that "we should read our Bibles more meaningfully," this message will have less involvement. You are more likely to change the attitudes of your audience from one latitude to another (e.g., from rejection to acceptance) when they have less involvement. Consider your audience's general latitude for the topic and their involvement in the issue as you analyze your audience.

Summary

A skilled speaker should begin preparation of a speech by conducting a thorough audience analysis. One should choose a relevant topic by examining demographics and decide how to present it by analyzing psychographics. By conducting a proper audience analysis, the speaker will be effective, and the audience will be edified. Indeed, this is the first, crucial step in a speech being audience-centered rather than speaker-centered.

6

FINDING A TOPIC

For many speakers, choosing a topic is half of the battle. From the thousands of Bible passages and the limitless number of applications, how can a speaker choose just one? Well, in light of the previous two chapters, the place to start should be evident: your audience! Skilled speakers analyze the needs and knowledge of their audience to choose a topic that is relevant for them. When Paul went to a synagogue in Acts 13, he spoke of David; when he went to the Areopagus in Acts 17, he spoke of the unknown god. How did Paul choose his topic? He considered his audience. Below we will offer further recommendations for choosing a topic and offer warnings of mistakes to avoid in this process.

Sources for Topic Selection

While the selection of your topic should begin with the needs and concerns of the audience, there are various sources to help you narrow it down. First, you may scope out the needs of your brethren by talking with them. Are there discouraged brethren who need an encouraging message about the victory of faith? Are there weak brethren who need a reminder of the perils of sin and the power of the gospel? Are there lost souls who need a clear message about the importance of the cross? Are there retired brethren who seek to be useful in the kingdom but lack direction? The possible topics are endless, and your chosen topic may not address everyone there, but get to know your audience and their needs.

What do you do if a topic is still not clear after thinking through your audience's needs? For example, you may preach at a church for the first time and not know anyone there. In this case, think through the universal messages of the gospel. Nearly every audience could benefit from a soul-stirring message on God's grace, and almost anyone would profit from a sober reminder of God's holiness. The gospel, by its nature, is universal, and any of these ubiquitous themes (e.g., the nature of God, the power of the gospel, the necessity of faith, the actions of a godly disciple, etc.) can provide powerful topics.

Furthermore, you may choose a topic or text about which you are passionate. If Hebrews 11.1 is your favorite verse, speak about the nature and the importance of faith in the Christian life. If Philippians 3.12–15 has helped you make it through tough times, explain the significance of endurance and growth in our spiritual journey. If you have recently been grieving over the loss of a loved one, present a comforting message to those who have gone through the same. If you have been working on using your tongue to God's glory, instruct others to do the same from James 3. Whatever you select, connect your passion to your audience's needs. On this note, reading will improve your topic selection skills. By considering multiple parts of the Bible, reading various types of literature, and even listening to skilled preachers and speakers, you may find motivation for speaking. Do not plagiarize another's message, but certainly learn from them and find motivation from their work.

The Goal of Your Message

As you choose your topic, carefully consider your message's goal. Paul instructed Timothy, "...preach the word; be ready in season and out of season; reprove, rebuke, and exhort, with complete patience and teaching" (2 Tim 4.2). At times we must reprove; at times we have to rebuke; and at times we need to exhort. As we explained above, knowing your audience and their needs will dictate your goal. If you realize that your audience contains various hurting hearts, perhaps it is time to exhort and encourage. If you see a weakness that needs to be corrected, you may need to rebuke. We must always "speak the truth in love," (Eph 4.15), no matter our goal. Some preachers thrive on negativity; others find comfort in positive messages. As a preacher of the gospel, you must overcome your personal inclinations and meet the needs of the audience, reproving, rebuking, and exhorting.

Topical and Textual Sermons

Preachers have generally divided sermons into either topical or textual sermons. While this may be helpful in narrowing down a sermon topic, we would argue that such a distinction may be artificial as every quality sermon should have both a text and a topic of focus. Rather than choosing between topical or textual, *good sermons usually discuss a topic in light of a text*. For example, if you choose to preach on the qualities that should define our daily walks with God (a topic), you could utilize Ephesians 4.1–6 (a text) to show how we are to "walk worthy of our calling" (v 1), with humility, gentleness, patience, love, and unity.

Perhaps more accurate a distinction concerns how many texts a sermon uses: one or many. Expository (or textual) preaching will stay grounded in one text, working the audience through the intricacies of the passage while topical sermons will connect various texts in an inductive fashion to make a more general point. Both have their place in preaching. For example, you could preach an expository sermon on contentment by analyzing 1 Timothy 6.3–10, or you could preach a topical sermon on contentment by drawing from 1 Timothy 6.3–10; Psalm 37.16; Philippians 4.10–13; and Hebrews 13.5 to demonstrate that true contentment comes from finding satisfaction in God. No matter how many texts you decide to use, always "rightly handle the Word of Truth" (2 Tim 2.15).

As a word of caution, avoid information overload when using multiple texts. New Testament writers often drew from the Old Testament Scriptures, but they did so purposefully and meaningfully. Some preachers verse their audiences to death, referencing so many passages that their audiences often forget the point of the message. If we may offer a preaching proverb: Better is one text rightly handled than a hundred texts loosely given!

Pitfalls in Topic Selection

We offer three warnings about topic selection. First, do not speak over your audience's head. You may have a passion for biology and want to explain how the intricacies of the human genome speak to the existence of God, but be careful that such a message does not go right over your audience's head and right out the door! Wait to tackle complex topics after you season your speaking skills. Second, avoid repetition of a recent talk from another brother. If the local evangelist has been concentrating on a Biblical series, avoid selecting a similar subject for a Wednesday evening talk. The Bible contains far too many topics to choose one recently preached on.

Finally, consider time limitations. Turning a five-minute talk into a fifteen-minute mini-sermon is usually greeted with frowns and fidgetiness. The solution is to limit the scope of the topic to fit the time limits. While many preachers bemoan the fact, the skilled speaker recognizes and adapts to the time limitations of an audience. From a learning perspective, an audience cannot comprehend a large amount of material in a short period of time. One of the rules most often broken by beginning speakers is *information overload*, where the speaker gives more information than the audience can retain.[13] This is especially true in Wednesday evening talks. Broad topics such as love, forgiveness, salvation, etc., are often selected for five-minute presentations, yet the result is a shallow treatment of a deep Biblical topic. When choosing a topic such as love for a Wednesday night talk, narrow it down to an aspect of love that results in a more satisfying subtopic. You could, for example, speak about love in action, as John elaborates on in 1 John 3.16–18. Love, he declares is seen when we provide for the needs of one another. Or, one might use the words of James 3 when he shows how contradictory our words can be when we both bless and curse with the same tongue. Whatever topic you choose, narrow it to fit the time limits but without including an overabundance of Scripture and biblical concepts. This may take time and experience, but in following this advice, you will find more satisfied and edified listeners.

7

GATHERING MATERIALS

While choosing a topic may be half the battle, it is just the beginning of crafting a quality speech. Your next step is to research your topic, after which you will begin writing the speech (which we will address in Chapter 8). Central to the research process is gathering supporting materials. Research can be time-consuming, but gathering adequate materials will strengthen your speech and its impact. To understand how to gather materials, we first must address some key aspects of *persuasion*.

The Toulmin Model

The purpose of research is not only to learn more about the topic but even more so to support your claims in the talk. The Toulmin Model, a useful tool for understanding how to support your claims, proposes that arguments consist of three critical parts: claim, data, and warrant.[14] The claim is the argument you are making; the data are the pieces of evidence you provide to support the claim; and the warrant is the logical justification for the argument. For example, if you make the claim, "Jesus is the only path to eternal salvation," you may provide Acts 4.12 as your data. If your audience accepts the authority of Scripture, then your claim would be warranted; however, if you are preaching to someone who does not accept the authority of Scripture, you would have to first argue that the Bible is truly the Word of God. *The Toulmin Model shows the importance of audience-centered persuasion, making claims that are warranted to your audience.* Yes, you must avoid logical fallacies (e.g., straw man, false dichotomy, post hoc ergo propter hoc, etc.) to make persuasive claims, but more importantly, you must ask what evidence you must provide to warrant your claims.

While the process of persuasion is complex, the Toulmin Model demonstrates that the key to successful argumentation lies in making warranted claims. Therefore, as you gather materials, you must gather sufficient evidence to support your claims, making them warranted in the minds of your audience. Some claims may require little evidence. For example, if you make the claim, "God expects purity in our lives," while speaking to a group of mature Christians, you may not even need evidence to make this claim warranted. However, if you are speaking to a new convert, you may need to point out 1 Thessalonians 4.1–8 as evidence to make the claim warranted. In summary, *provide sufficient evidence to warrant your claims.*

Types of Evidence

As you consider the evidence you need in your speech, you should also give thought to the form of evidence you provide. Aristotle famously offered three forms of persuasive appeals: ethos, pathos, and logos.[15] Ethos refers to an appeal to the speaker's character; pathos refers to an appeal to emotion; and logos refers to an appeal to reason. All three have their unique argumentative power. In light of the Toulmin Model, the task for you as a speaker is to determine which form of persuasive appeal will warrant your claim. If you claim that profanity is a widespread problem in America today, a logos appeal using statistics of profanity in films would warrant your claim. If you claim that profanity has negative consequences, a pathos appeal using a story of someone hurt by damaging words would warrant your claim. If you claim that your audience should give up profanity, an ethos appeal to your own victory over sin would warrant your claim. In summary, *consider your claim and what form of persuasive appeal would warrant it.*

The Bible as Evidence

Giving thought to both the claims you are making and the form of evidence needed to warrant them, you now can begin your research process. The greatest resource you have for any talk or sermon is the Bible. As Paul boldy declared, "All Scripture is breathed out by God and profitable for teaching, for reproof, for correction, and for training in righteousness, that the man of God may be complete, equipped for every good work" (2 Tim 3.16–17). You can fill your sermon with heart-wrenching stories and infallible statistics, but no sermon is adequate unless the Bible is central. Our words should simply be a vehicle for communicating the greater Word of God.

Other Sources for Supporting Materials

While the Bible should always be central in your preaching, you may find it useful to reference other materials as you conduct your research; there are two general types of resources you will utilize in your preparation. First, Bible study aids can, when used appropriately, improve your handling of God's Word. Especially for topical sermons (i.e., those that draw from multiple texts), concordances and books such as *Nave's Topical Bible* can be useful for researching relevant Bible passages. Online Bibles and Bible study tools can also be helpful toward this end. Bible dictionaries and Greek interlinears may be helpful, but use them wisely. Citing the meaning of Hebrew or Greek words can be dangerous if you have only a basic knowledge of the languages. If you do not know them, stick to English resources. Representing ourselves as experts of the languages when we are not can backfire and harm our handling of God's Word. Commentaries, Christian literature, and online sermons can also enrich our understanding of God's Word. Of course, always weigh their claims with the standard of Scripture, and cite your sources when applicable. Your Bible study skills will improve with practice, but dig into the depth of God's Word!

Second, you may consult extra-biblical sources to support your claims. More successful talks and sermons have at least a sprinkling of specifics. Rather than saying, "Lots of Americans believe...," use sources to support your claims with specifics. If you are seeking evidence for a claim concerning the religious trends of America, you may research

Gathering Materials | 45

statistics from sites like the Barna Group, an organization that conducts research on religious trends. If you are seeking evidence for the marriage rates in America, you may look at analysis from the Pew Research Center. If you are looking for a pathos appeal, you may tell a moving story you read in the newspaper. Books, newspapers, magazines, blogs, research centers, and even personal stories can all provide sources for your research.

We offer three recommendations (i.e., the three Cs) when using resources other than the Bible for your research. First, use them **correctly**. Do not take a story out of context, and never twist data to fit your point. Rather, let the data lead to your conclusions. Second, check the **credibility** of your sources. Data analysts often joke that ninety percent of statistics are made up. If you are using a statistic or fact, ensure the source is reliable and accurate. If you are using a story, check that the source is trustworthy. Your credibility as a speaker relies on the credibility of your sources. Finally, **cite** your sources. Doing so increases your ethos as a speaker and is fair to the sources that you used.

SECTION THREE

Organization

8

Organizing Your Message

The Importance of Organization

While organization is frequently minimized or even forgotten in the process of preparing Bible talks, it is as important as the content and in some ways more important than delivery. Poorly organized talks and sermons lose the audience's attention and interest, prevent the audience from understanding the flow of the message, and even hinder the audience from remembering anything that is said after the talk is completed. Thus, when organization is forsaken, all three main purposes of Biblical talks are obstructed (i.e., attention, comprehension, and retention). On the other hand, well-organized talks allow the speaker to lead an audience's minds through a clear message that will impact their lives and stay with them. Furthermore, each of the great sermons in Acts has a central claim and a clear organizational pattern, and we should learn from these examples.

The Process of Organization

Organized speeches have four main parts: an introduction, a thesis statement, a body, and a conclusion.[16] While a final speech should work toward this order, the actual process of preparing a well-organized talk differs. Indeed, the *preparation order* for Bible talks is this: thesis, body, conclusion, and introduction.

While this preparation order may seem counterintuitive, it is truly the most useful for the speech-preparation process. Furthermore, seasoned speakers recognize that the process of speech preparation is often messy and rather non-linear. However, following this recommended order will yield a better-organized, more impactful speech. Let us explain. Often speakers (and writers) like to begin with the introduction. However, this does not make sense because you really do not yet have anything to introduce. However, if a speaker first prepares the body, the introduction should be simple and more effective to write.

Thesis

Most critical to the process of organization and preparation in general is the construction of the thesis statement, which is a single, simple declarative sentence that summarizes the whole message. Without a clear thesis statement, talks are usually ineffective as they are difficult to understand and follow. With a clear thesis statement, the speaker is mindful of what he wants the listeners to understand, to believe, or to do. For example, if you have decided to speak on the topic of redemption, a thesis statement could be, "Without a Redeemer, there is no salvation." This simple statement will allow you to remain focused while preparing the rest of the talk and also allow the listeners to understand the purpose of the lesson clearly. As you prepare your

Organizing Your Message | 51

talk, you may adjust your thesis statement as you discover and think through new ideas, but the final thesis statement should clearly reflect the basic message of the talk.

Body

After constructing the thesis statement, the next logical step is to outline the main section of your talk, the body. The most important principle to remember during this step is that all parts of the body should relate back to the thesis statement. Beginning speakers often include everything they know about a topic in a talk, even if it does not support or even relate to the thesis statement. Avoid this temptation! Rather, organize your main points, subpoints, and all content around the thesis statement. If a part of the body does not relate to the thesis statement, reserve it for another talk.

During this second stage, you should begin by outlining your main points. Chapter 9 will demonstrate various organizational strategies, but remember that the purpose of the main points is to provide Biblical reasons to support the thesis statement. Outline all of your ideas in a logical fashion. Each main point needs elaboration to enhance understanding in the audience. Reference Appendix B for a demonstration of this outlining strategy.

For example, your thesis statement may be, "Without a Redeemer, there is no salvation." The two main points could be as follows: (1) Redemption saves one from a lost state and (2) Redemption requires a Redeemer. From here, you would outline subpoints and choose supporting materials (i.e., Biblical passages, quotations from scholars, illustrations, etc.) to support your thesis statement.

Conclusion

The third major step in the preparation process is to develop an ending to your message. Its purpose is to wrap up and give a sense of completeness to the talk. Many beginning speakers often end by what we call the "meat cleaver" approach, which is just stopping the speech by saying, "That's it." However, an effective conclusion has the power to lead hearts to action and hearers to Christ. Chapter 10 will give more details about conclusions and introductions, but remember their purpose is to provide a final clarifying message to the thesis statement and to lead the audience to action.

Introductions

The final step is to draft an introduction, which has two main purposes: to grab the audience's attention and to alert the listeners of the upcoming topic. Chapter 10 provides further explanation of effective introductions, but their importance in the talk cannot be underestimated. Effective introductions will captivate an audience's attention and clearly lead them into the body of the talk.

Putting It All Together

After going through the preparation order for Bible talks, you then change the order on the presentation outline. The final order should be introduction, thesis statement, body, and conclusion. Appendix B offers a sample outline for reference, and following this outline format assures that the talk is well organized and flows smoothly. Speeches should be fluid in their design and delivery, and effective outlines contribute greatly to this outcome. Also, note the transitions between each of the major sections as clear transitions allow the speaker and the audience to see the flow of the speech. Indeed, effective organization will lead to attention, comprehension, and retention of a Bible talk.

9

ORGANIZATIONAL PATTERNS

How Many Main Points?

As explained in chapter 8, not only should the overall speech be well organized, but the body should be organized with clear main points, the purpose of which is to support or prove the thesis of the talk. Frequently students are taught in high school English classes that any essay or speech should have three main points. While this advice may be useful for beginners, it is simply unrealistic and ineffective for Bible talks and sermons. So how many points should a Bible talk have? Enough to make the point! Moreover, every talk should have at least two main points, but the actual number depends on the speaker and the topic. We usually have two main points but sometimes have as many as four. Three has no superiority to other numbers, but each talk should have enough main points to support or prove the thesis.

The Limitation of Topical Outlines

From our experience in listening to preachers, most sermons utilize a topical outline, meaning the talk has an overarching theme and main points that relate in different ways to that theme. [Note: The term "topical" in this case refers to a topical organizational pattern, not a "topical" (as opposed to textual) sermon.] As an example of the topical outline, a thesis may be, "Christians should be holy." Main point (MP) 1 would be "Holiness in Thought"; MP2 would be "Holiness in Action"; and MP3 would be "Holiness in Speech." Moreover, this centers around the concept of holiness, and the main points discuss different aspects of lived holiness.

While the topical outline has its place at times, it has two main limitations. First, the audience fails to grasp a clear takeaway. Such topical sermons often try to preach everything without saying anything! In the holiness example, the sermon discusses displays of holiness without ever truly explaining the meaning of holiness; thus, an audience would not truly understand the impact of holiness on their lives through this talk. Second, the main points don't relate to each other. The most effective talks integrate their main points into a seamless argument while topical outlines contain main points that share a theme but really do not relate to form a larger argument. Below we will show you various organizational patterns to overcome these two limitations.

Organizational Patterns

When choosing an organizational pattern, you should select the one that best proves or supports your thesis. Furthermore, when writing the main points, consider not only what they should be but also how they relate to one another. You want your main points to form an overarching argument, leaving your audience with a clear understanding of your thesis. This argument can be formed deductively or inductively.

Deduction. Deduction argues from broad statements to a specific conclusion. In a deductive argument, you combine two claims (also called premises) to make a specific conclusion. A famous deductive argument goes as follows: "All men are mortal. Aristotle is a man. Therefore, Aristotle is mortal." The burden of a speaker using deduction is to ensure the argument is valid and to prove the two premises to the audience.

Within Bible talks, deduction can be a powerful tool. Returning to the concept of holiness in a sermon, a speaker can have a more strongly supported thesis by claiming, "Christians should be holy." *MP1: God is holy. MP2: Christians should be like God. Conclusion: Therefore, Christians should be holy.* In such as sermon, the speaker not only connects the concept of holiness to the nature of God but also demonstrates the importance and the implications of holiness through sound argumentation. Such a structure can have greater impact than the aforementioned topical example.

Induction. The other type of argumentation is induction, in which a speaker uses more specific claims to reach a broader conclusion. The speaker reasons through various observations toward a warranted conclusion. The burden on the speaker is to provide enough evidence to ensure the claim is warranted. Returning to the holiness example, the thesis is "Christians should be holy." In an inductive pattern, main points could be as follows: *MP1: Holiness is commanded in the Bible. MP2: The pitfalls of unholiness are severe and should be avoided. MP3: Holiness provides reward in this life and the life to come.* In such a pattern, the speaker recognizes that the individual points may not be enough to convince an audience of the final conclusion; however, taken together, they have the strength to persuade the audience. The speaker must reason through each of the individual main points, which will then lead the audience to viewing the final claim as warranted. While there are various types of inductive patterns, below are the ones that are most useful in Bible talks and sermons.[17] Each will be illustrated using the thesis "Christians should be holy."

Opposing Points. The speaker contrasts two opposing sides of an issue or concept. For example, a speaker may illustrate the pros in MP1 and the cons in MP2; the good in MP1 and the evil in MP2; etc. The two main points should be antithetical to each other. *MP1: God requires holiness of His people. MP2: Satan deceives us into unholy action.*

Complementary. The speaker integrates two similar sides of a topic. For example, a speaker may want to compare two aspects of a Biblical issue. The key to the complementary pattern is to compare the main points and not leave them as separate thoughts, as often happens with the topical pattern. *MP1: Holiness derives from God's nature. MP2: Holiness is demonstrated through human thought and action.*

Organizational Patterns | 59

Chronological. The speaker traces a Biblical concept through various times. Stephen used this pattern in Acts 7, tracing the theme of rejection through Jewish history. Such a pattern allows the audience to see the development of a concept through history. *MP1: God required ritual sanctification during the Old Testament. MP2: God requires spiritual sanctification during the New Testament.*

Cause-Effect. The speaker argues either from a cause to an effect or from an effect to a cause. In either case, a speaker must demonstrate a warranted connection between the cause and the effect. *MP1: Holiness derives from being like God. MP2: Being like God results in pure actions.*

Problem-Solution. The speaker focuses on a specific problem, explaining how to solve it. This is a useful strategy in dealing with topics relating to sin as it not only highlights what the problem is, but it also provides a solution for the hearers. *MP1: Sinful action separates us from God. MP2: We should separate ourselves from the ways of the world unto godly behavior.*

Narrative. The speaker tells a story throughout the sermon, arriving at an illustrated point. Though this is not often used in contemporary preaching, it is consistent with the parables of Jesus. Narratives contain a purpose, a plot, characters, and dialogue. These can either be Biblical stories, expounded on in the sermon, or other illustrations to make a spiritual point. The main points are the highlights of the story. *MP1: God made man in His image. MP2: Man and woman were in fellowship with God in the garden. MP3: Man and woman sinned. MP4: Man and woman were separated from the presence of God. MP5: God promised a unity that would be brought through His seed.*

Topical. The speaker demonstrates a theme in various contexts. While we warned of the overuse of the topical outline above, it certainly has its uses. If a speaker desires to show the vastness of a topic or the immense implications of a concept, topical can be useful. Again, make sure to connect your main points to a central thesis. *MP1: We should be holy in thought. MP2: We should be holy in action. MP3: We should be holy in speech.*

10

Introductions and Conclusions

The Importance of the Beginning and End

While introductions and conclusions should never consume a speech's time, they are critical to any speech's effectiveness. As we discussed in Chapter 4, all Bible talks have three general purposes: *attention, comprehension, and retention.* As a reminder, a Bible talk should grab an audience's focus (attention); lead to understanding in the audience's mind (comprehension); and facilitate prolonged learning with the audience (retention). Introductions and conclusions are critical to the success of all three major purposes of a Bible talk.

Introductions are most critical to grabbing the audience's attention but can also aid comprehension and retention. On the other hand, conclusions are most critical to facilitating retention but can likewise aid attention and comprehension. Below we will further explain the functions of introductions and conclusions within Bible talks, granting special focus to how to craft skilled ones within the speech.

Introductions

Introductions serve many functions within a speech. Primarily, they gain the audience's attention. While we may assume that our audience is always ready to listen to the Word of God, brethren often are distracted at the beginning of the talk. Our task as we begin is to take their minds away from Sunday dinner or the cute baby two rows in front of them to a message from God's Word. Thus, effective introductions should begin with an attention getter, a section at the very beginning of the speech to grab the audience's attention. *Attention getters can take various forms,* but always make sure that it is appropriate to the occasion and relevant to the speech:

- **Story:** One of the most effective introductions is narrative. We are storytelling creatures, and stories can draw an audience's attention and engage their emotions at the beginning of a talk.[18] Stories should be short and appropriate to the audience's demographics. Recent events can often make effective introductions.

- **Interesting Quotation:** Quotations are effective when interesting and novel. As a general rule, you will grab your audience's attention better with shorter, easier to remember quotations than complicated ones.

- **Interesting Fact:** Like quotations, facts can likewise grab an audience's attention, yet the key word of this form of attention getter is interesting. Analyze your audience, and try to project what they would find interesting. You do not want to begin your talk with boring your audience to indifference. Shocking statements are effective here. People react more positively to new information than to old information.

- **Visual Aid**: You could likewise hold up an object, or show one on a PowerPoint slide. Of course, anything you say or show must be related to your topic. Never use something just for shock value when it is unrelated to your topic or thesis statement. That is called an unrelated introduction and results in confusion and disappointment.

While we generally recommend all of the previous forms of attention getters, there are also *attention getters to avoid:*

- **Prolonged Greetings**: While it is kind to welcome an audience and thank them for their presence, prolonged greetings often lose the audience's attention before you arrive at your main message. Be welcoming, but be brief. We recommend often including these short greetings after the attention getter itself.
- **Questions**: If we had to choose the attention getter that speakers, especially preachers, most overuse, it would be questions. As a speaker, you are there to answer questions, not raise them. Asking questions creates an awkward silence with the audience and is rarely ever effective as an attention getter.
- **Trite Sayings**: "Turn in your Bible to…" is almost an obligatory first sentence for most preachers, yet pre-

dictable sayings are usually not very attention-getting. Yes, always direct your audience to God's Word in your talk, but first grab the audience's attention so that God's Word can have its full impact.

- **Jokes:** While humor is often an effective speaking tool, it rarely belongs in an introduction. Jokes often give a tone of irreverence when placed at the very beginning of a talk.

As we recommended in chapter 8, write the introduction last in your preparation process. After thinking of an effective attention getter, the rest of your introduction should flow naturally. *Structure your introduction with the following important sections:*

- **Attention Getter:** As we emphasized above, choose an effective attention getter to begin the speech.
- **Introduce the Topic:** In addition to gaining audience attention, your introductory statements should alert your listeners to the upcoming topic. Remember, at this point in your message, listeners are in the dark. Everything you say or do should gradually open their minds to the topic you've prepared. Once they "get the drift," they are more prepared to listen.
- **Rationale:** After grabbing your audience's attention, explain how your message impacts them, providing a warrant for why they should listen. Doing so will increase your audience's engagement.
- **Forecast the Talk:** Finally, effective introductions often include a message about the message. It is

called forecasting. Listeners are then provided a preview of what you will cover. Not only do they now have a list or ideas to look for, but you also have raised your ethos because you are perceived as prepared. It is one of three cardinal rules of effective speaking: prepare, prepare, prepare!

In summary, introductions should grab an audience's attention and prepare them to comprehend and retain the message you are about to give. Introductions set the tone for the rest of the speech and can determine the effectiveness of the rest of the talk. In addition, introductions establish your personal ethos (or credibility) as a speaker, especially when you are speaking to new audiences. Audiences are more likely to listen to and accept information from a credible speaker, so you want to begin your talk with a strong perceived credibility, so that you can magnify the greater strength of God's Word in the rest of your talk.

Conclusions

Last but certainly not least is the conclusion, during which you will have a final chance to bring your speech to a smooth, effective finish. Effective conclusions are simple, memorable, and relatively short while ineffective conclusions are complex, forgettable, and drawn out. As a general rule, you do not want to introduce new information in the conclusion; rather, you should summarize and connect to what you have already said. As we stated above, the conclusion is critical to the audience's retention, so you will want to bring your main point to an understandable close. As with introductions, you generally want to avoid prolonged conclusions or farewells, questions, trite sayings, and jokes. Instead, we recommend one of the following *forms of conclusions:*

- **Restatement of main points:** A simple reminder of the main points of the speech will often improve an audience's retention of the message. Audiences generally appreciate and often need reminders of the thesis by the conclusion, so a short, simple restatement of main points can be an effective way to end.

- **Connection to the attention getter:** While we recommended writing the conclusion before the introduction in chapter 8, you may create an attention getter in your preparation process that you would like to reemphasize in the conclusion, increasing the audience's connection with the main message of your talk.

- **Call to action:** This is the most common among preachers, calling the audience to obey the Lord's invitation to salvation. You can also connect this invitation to the central thesis of your talk. For example, if you are speaking about "Living as Lights in a Dark World," your call to action could urge the audience to come to salvation in God, the Creator of light. This can create a persuasive call to response in your audience's minds.

SECTION FOUR

Delivery

11

CONTROLLING YOUR FEAR

The Frequency of Fear

Fear of public speaking is the most common barrier to presenting Bible talks. While beginning speakers often feel alone in their fear of public speaking, we can assure you that fear is universal. As collegiate speech teachers, we have seen fear of public speaking in countless students. We have seen students put off our class until they are seniors, hyperventilate in their speeches, completely forget their speeches, and even become physically sick at the thought of a speech. While fear itself may be nearly ubiquitous, you can avoid these drastic responses to fear with proper training.

Approach or Avoidance

The fear of public speaking is so common that communication scholars have given it a formal name, public speaking anxiety (PSA).[19] When confronted with PSA, speakers often have a fight or flight reaction, what social scientists call approach or avoidance.[20] Moreover, when we experience PSA, we can either approach it (i.e., continue with the speech in spite of the fear) or avoid it (i.e., shut down the speech in the face of fear). Below we will teach you how to approach rather than avoid a speech when faced with PSA.

PSA has various sources, yet we generally experience it when we consider everything that could go wrong in a speech. What if I forget what I am supposed to say? What if I make a mistake? What if everyone thinks I've done a bad job? What if no one pays attention? What if a bird flies inside the building and takes page three of my notes (ok…that may be a bit extreme, but you get the picture!)? We must approach, rather than avoid, these fears if we are to overcome PSA.

Franklin D. Roosevelt, in his first inaugural address in 1933, uttered the now famous phrase, "…the only thing we have to fear is fear itself."[21] Although he was trying to console a nation in the throes of the Great Depression, his words provide us wisdom for public speaking. Rarely do our worst fears come true, so we must avoid the downfalls of PSA. However, a certain amount of anxiety can actually be helpful. Fear, or the Biblical companion reverence, teaches us the importance of what we are about to do: speak the Word of God. Fear, in the appropriate quantity, can fire up our mind and body and keep us mentally engaged through the rush of adrenaline. The lack of fear can lead to arrogance in the pulpit, and too much fear can lead to a debilitating delivery. Thus, we are not teaching you to avoid fear completely; rather, we are teaching you to approach it with reverence so that you can learn to *control* PSA.

Strategies for Controlling Fear

Although the total avoidance of fear is both unrealistic and unwise, we will teach you various strategies for controlling extreme levels of fear below. Some may be more helpful for you than others.

Faith. Just as Moses faced PSA when he spoke to God at the burning bush (Exod 3), we must trust in God to carry us through any fear. As Psalm 56.3 declares, "When I am afraid, I put my trust in you." God wants us to succeed as we preach His Word, and only trust in Him will allow us to approach any fear. With His power to give us resolve and strength, there is little to fear; we must pray in faith to Him.

Encouragement from Brethren. On the whole, brothers and sisters in Christ want young men to succeed in their talks. Just as you are "building up the body of Christ" (Eph 4.12) in your talks, brethren will build you up with encouraging words afterward. While we may fear the judgment of brethren, our experience has demonstrated the kindness of most. Sure, you will receive criticism, but use it as an opportunity for improvement and growth as a speaker.

Overcome Projection. Projection is a psychological effect, occurring when we assign our own thoughts and feelings to others.[22] For example, if I am nervous before a talk, I will project my nervousness on others and assume that everyone else is nervous to hear me. As we said above, most brethren want you to do well and speak to the glory of God. Don't psych yourself out before you even get up to speak.

Prepare, Prepare, Prepare. If you play an instrument, you know that it requires hundreds of hours to become skilled with it; even after you are skilled, it can still take hours to learn a new piece. Speaking is no different. While talking comes naturally to us as children, skilled speaking takes time to develop. While an invitation may last about five minutes, you should still put hours into the research, writing, editing, and practicing. Sufficient preparation can help alleviate the extreme amounts of fear.

Memorize the Introduction. From experience, we will tell you that the introduction will make or break a talk. While we recommend extemporaneous delivery (which we address in another chapter) for the body of a speech, memorizing the introduction can help beginning speakers. If you provide a smooth introduction, the rest of the speech should follow naturally.

Choose an Appropriate Topic. When you learn to ride a bike, you start with training wheels before trying to ride on one wheel. Likewise, begin with topics that you are able to present well. In other words, don't go over your head! Choosing to speak, for example, on the role of the Holy Spirit in the Christian's life, the book of Revelation, or baptism of the dead would probably not be ideal topics for new speakers. Simplicity does not imply redundancy. Relatively well-known spiritual needs can still be presented in fresh, compelling ways. Using topics in which you feel competent reduces your fear.

Imagined Interaction. This is a fancy phrase meaning that you imagine yourself in the actual speaking situation.²³ For example, if you are preparing an invitation, imagine yourself looking over the faces of the brethren before you speak. Imagine the atmosphere of the room, the looks on people's faces, the sounds of pages turning, etc. As another method, you can also ask to practice from the pulpit a week or two before you present. Such practice will alleviate fear.

Deep Breathing. Right before you speak, perhaps the best step you can take, besides prayer, is deep breathing. Relax the lower part of your abdomen while you breathe, and take in several slow, deep breaths. Doing so will calm your nerves and provide you a smooth speaking voice.

Speak Slowly. When we experience PSA, we often speak quickly. Speak slower than normal as you begin your talk, and you will calm your nerves and allow your audience to understand you. I (Ryan) struggled with pace when I was first learning to speak, so I would write "TALK SLOWLY!" at the top of my outlines. Such a note forced me to slow down, and my speaking improved because of it.

Avoid PowerPoint. While we will provide recommendations for visual aids in a following chapter, we generally recommend that beginning speakers avoid PowerPoint. Visual aids, while important, often distract new speakers, making them nervous. Become a competent speaker, and then add in visual aids. If you decide to use them, keep them simple.

Act Confident. Never admit your nervousness to an audience; rather, act confident. When you speak God's utterances and use His strength, He will be glorified (1 Pet

4.11). Confidence will increase the impact of your message and reduce your nerves.

12

VERBAL DELIVERY AND LANGUAGE

After working through the content and organization of the speech, it is time to consider the delivery. You have chosen your topic, conducted your research, selected the supporting materials, and outlined the speech. Now you must put your thoughts into words. In this chapter, we will explain how to format your speaking notes and how to present your speech with effective language.

Formatting Your Notes

As you prepare your speech, you will need to decide how to format your speaking notes. Consider both the length of the speech and also its location. For a short invitation, you may decide to condense your outline to note cards, maximizing your eye contact with your audience; if you use note cards, make sure to number them. For a full-length sermon at the pulpit, you may decide to use a full outline on 8.5"x11" paper. Below are various methods of formatting your speaking notes:

- **Manuscript**: With a manuscript, you present your speech from a word-for-word paper. While politicians often use these, we recommend against them for most sermons. Unless you have a teleprompter, manuscripts significantly reduce eye contact and your connection with the audience. As we recommended in Chapter 11, you may decide to use a manuscript for your introduction, but be cautious of using them for the whole speech.

- **Impromptu**: With impromptu speaking, you use no notes, rather presenting the speech on the spot. Unless you are called upon at a moment's notice to preach, never rely on impromptu for Bible talks or sermons. Rather, put in the necessary preparation before the speech.

- **Extemporaneous**: For most situations, we recommend extemporaneous style, in which a speaker utilizes a speaking outline to present. Such outlines may be very detailed or relatively brief, depending on the experience and personal preferences of the speaker. You can use various formatting techniques to make the outline easy to follow in the presentation: putting keywords in bold, using large fonts for transitions or key phrases, underlining important verses, highlighting summaries, etc. Fluid organization and clear formatting can make the outline easy to read during the presentation, leading to a smooth delivery. See Appendix B for a sample outline.

The Goals of Language

As God has spoken to us through the Word (John 1.1–2; Heb 1.1–2), we must speak through words. Such a recognition may sound self-evident, but it highlights the importance of language to our talks. Indeed, Solomon said, "To make an apt answer is a joy to a man, and a word in season, how good it is!" (Prov 15.23). As you craft your speech, you should give careful attention to the words you choose. Perhaps the most important recommendation we can give is the following: *write for the ear, not the eye*. The way you write a paper should be different from the way you write a speech outline. Listeners, unlike readers, cannot go back over materials or "rehear" portions of the message. Thus, your language should present your thoughts so that your audience can understand the message. To do so, you should consider the following goals of language: clarity, vividness, conciseness, and appropriateness.[24]

Clarity

To maximize your audience's understanding of the message, you should use clear language. Clarity relies on anticipating the connotative definition of a word. While denotation is the literal, dictionary meaning of a word, connotation is the personal, subjective meaning that people assign to words. Skilled speakers choose words with reference to words' expected connotations.

Consider, for example, the word *baptism*. While the word may literally mean immersion, some audience members may give different personal meanings to the word: sprinkling, pouring, baptism of the Spirit, or perhaps immersion. If you want an audience to picture immersion, perhaps using that word instead of baptism would be clearer to your audience.

Connected to connotations, consider using words that are more specific than general. Avoid such abstract words as "a lot," "big," "bad," etc. Rather, use words that are concrete. As an example, think of how many connotations people assign to love: affection, emotional warmth, pleasure, etc. Rather than just talking about the love of God on the cross, you may want to first discuss the selfless love God showed on the cross. Such specificity enhances the clarity of your speech. On this note, try to anticipate whether your audiences will know the specific words you are using. If you introduce unfamiliar terms, define them, establishing the denotation of the term.

Vividness

As you seek to achieve clarity, vividness through imagery can aid you. Imagery paints word pictures that tell stories in your audience's minds. Jesus used imagery in His preaching, with parables frequenting His teaching (Matt 13.10–17). Rather than just explaining the different types of hearts and how they receive the gospel, Jesus used the imagery of a sower. Such imagery increased the vividness of His message. Likewise, using analogies, metaphors, comparisons, and contrasts can all improve the vividness of your language. To illustrate our point, a sermon without imagery is like a kale salad without salad dressing while a sermon with imagery is like a kale salad tossed in a tasty balsamic vinaigrette; both salads are good for you while the latter is more appealing and helps the food to go down.

Conciseness

Apart from clarity and vividness, conciseness can also improve your language use. Indeed, choosing the fewest correct words to make your point is far preferable to long-winded ramblings. As Thomas Jefferson said, "The most valuable of all talents is that of never using two words where one will do."[25]

Appropriateness

All language should be appropriate to the audience, the speaker, and the occasion. Common sense should prevail, and accurate audience analysis is mandatory. As an example, your audience should dictate the language you use when preaching on sexual sins. The language of this sermon should be different from when you preach to an audience of adults versus an audience including young children. Think through words' connotations, and avoid ones that your audience will view as inappropriate.

Considering an audience's gender, political beliefs, cultural backgrounds, biases, and even biblical beliefs can help you in choosing appropriate language. As a couple of examples, even saying *firefighter* instead of *fireman* may seem more appropriate to your audience and avoid distractions. Likewise, on your PowerPoints, capitalizing pronouns for God (e.g., He, His, Him, etc.) may appear more appropriate to some audience members than not doing so. If you are preaching to a multicultural audience, also be aware of colloquial expressions and the potential confusion they can bring. As a final note on appropriateness, personal pronouns (e.g., I, my, we, etc.) are certainly appropriate for sermons. Such pronouns can make your message more personable and conversational.

13

NONVERBAL DELIVERY

Nonverbal communication plays an important role in the communication process, yet its importance must not be exaggerated. At times we hear such made-up statistics such as, "Communication is 93% nonverbal and 7% verbal." Such figures exaggerate the importance of nonverbal communication.[26] As we have argued in previous chapters, the focus in any speech should be the message/content, not the delivery.

As a note, by *verbal*, we mean "said with words," and by *nonverbal*, we mean "said without words." Verbal communication must be distinguished from vocal communication, which concerns how the verbal message is said with the voice. Technically, vocal communication is a form of nonverbal communication. Below we will explain the functions of nonverbal communication within a speech and how to craft effective nonverbal communication.

The Functions of Nonverbal Communication

Nonverbal communication serves various roles within a communication episode.[27]

- **Repeating**: Some nonverbal cues can simply echo what you say verbally. For example, nodding your head while saying, "yes" repeats the verbal message.
- **Conflicting**: On the contrary, nonverbal cues can also contradict a verbal message. For example, if you say, "I'm fine" while frowning, your facial expression contradicts your verbal message.
- **Complementing**: Nonverbal cues can also modify the interpretation of a verbal message. For example, if you clap your hands while exclaiming, "Great!" then your gestures complement your verbal message.
- **Substituting**: Nonverbal cues can take the place of verbal messages. Rather than saying, "yes," you may just nod your head.
- **Accenting**: Nonverbal cues can intensify or moderate a verbal message. For example, giving a friend a hug while expressing condolences would intensify the verbal messages.
- **Regulating**: Finally, nonverbal cues may regulate an interaction. By using gestures like a hand wave or posture like leaning in, you can speed up or slow down an interaction.

Being aware of the functions of nonverbal communication within a speech allows you to craft messages with power and skill. For example, you may decide to substitute a gesture for "Come forward" when offering the invitation, providing a memorable plea. You may decide to complement a powerful point by changing your posture and using a loud tone. You may decide to demonstrate the irony of sin by using a conflicting verbal and nonverbal message. However you use them, your nonverbal cues should be effective and further the audience's understanding of your message.

Forms of Nonverbal Communication

Aside from their functions, nonverbal cues can also take various forms.[28] Some are more obvious than others, but speakers can use them all effectively to present their message.

- **Vocalics**: While we will discuss vocalics—the use of the voice in a speech—in detail in the next chapter, its importance merits a mention here. Many churches audio record their messages, so pay special attention to your vocalics and how they relate to the verbal message.

- **Eye Contact**: Good speakers connect with their audience through eye contact. It is unwise to look at only one person or one section of the auditorium. Rather, skilled speakers use what we call the "windshield wiper technique," meaning you sweep your eyes back and forth across the entire audience. When you first arrive at the pulpit, take a moment to sweep the audience, connecting with them and alerting them to your readiness to speak.

- **Facial Expressions**: No matter the size of the auditorium, an audience will look at your face more than any other part of your body as you speak. Your facial expressions should complement and accent your verbal messages. They can communicate assurance, embarrassment, humor, empathy, anger, sadness, happiness, and a wide range of emotions.

- **Body Language and Gestures**: Body language refers to movement of any part of the body (e.g., head, face, torso, hands, arms, and feet) while gestures refer specifically to movement of the hands and arms. Both can be used for impact within the talk. While we do not recommend formalized gestures as were common in the Elocutionary Movement (i.e., an eighteenth century British movement that emphasized systematic nonverbal movements), we recommend purposeful gestures that complement your verbal messages. Never distract your audience with overdone body language; subtlety is often key.

- **Space**: While we may not give it as much thought as the other forms of nonverbal communication, space can play a powerful role in the communication process. Audiences generally hold expectations for the preacher to stand behind the pulpit. As a beginning speaker, it is best to follow these expectations; however, as you advance in skill, you may decide to violate their spatial expectations, complementing a verbal message to make a powerful point, by moving from behind the pulpit.

- **Physical Appearances**: Finally, your physical appearances also send nonverbal cues. You never want your physical appearances to conflict with your verbal messages; rather, minimize distractions so that your message can shine through.

14

Vocal Delivery

As we mentioned in the previous chapter, verbal communication concerns the words you use while nonverbal communication concerns how you say these words. Above all, strive for *clarity* in your delivery. While it may take time to find your voice as a speaker, always pursue clarity in your vocal delivery. Remember that the content, not the delivery, should be the focus of the speech; delivery is just the conduit through which you present the content. Paul himself did not seek "lofty speech" (1 Cor 2.1), rather focusing on a clear presentation of the gospel message.

As you seek clarity in your speech, consider the following aspects of vocal delivery:[29]

- **Rate/Tempo**: Rate concerns how quickly or slowly you speak. Beginning speakers normally speak too quickly for audiences to understand, so slow your rate down. Such will help the audience to comprehend your message.

- **Volume**: You should speak loud enough for your audience to hear you. Both moments of loud speech and soft speech can be used for dramatic effect, but seek a normal speaking voice that is easy to hear.

- **Pitch and Tone**: Your voice should be strong but not booming. While low-pitched voices sound authoritative and high-pitched voices sound excited, your normal pitch should sound relaxed. Depending on your God-given voice, you may need to lower or raise your pitch for the sake of clarity.

- **Vocal Variety**: While a clear pitch is important, try not to remain at just one pitch, which can become monotonous. Voices that purposefully vary pitch are more interesting and can contribute to your dynamism as a speaker. Vocal variety can demonstrate power and conviction. Work toward purposeful, impactful inflections in your voice.

- **Rhythm**: Your speaking should be fluid, rather than stilted. Using musical terminology, legato (i.e., connected utterances) is preferable to staccato (i.e., disconnected utterances). Good speakers have flow between their words and between their sentences. Such creates a fluid speech.

- **Articulation**: Skilled speakers enunciate their words for their audience to hear. Mumbling is your enemy. Emphasize words for impact, but enunciate every word clearly.

- **Vocal Fillers**: Finally, avoid vocal fillers (e.g., um, uh, etc.). Adequate preparation and knowledge of your speech will reduce vocal fillers. As a speaking drill, practice your speech, starting from the beginning each time you use a vocal filler. Such practice will make you mindful when you use them.

Rehearsing Your Message

After developing your speaking outline, practice, practice, practice! Such practice will reduce your public speaking anxiety and better prepare you for your speech. We offer three recommendations for practice. First, contrary to the popular wisdom that "practice makes perfect," unguided practice may only cement bad habits. While we commend practice, we urge speakers to seek guidance and feedback as they practice; such is the reason that coaches are used in athletic sports. For example, if you practice your speech with a rapid rate but do not realize your speed, such repetition of the rate will cement it for when you present. Take the feedback of others as a means of improvement.

Second, go over your lesson multiple times. The more you go over your material, the more you will remember. As we recommended in the previous chapter, you may even practice at your church building. Do not leave this practice to the day before you present; rather, begin as early as possible, allowing you time to improve weaknesses as you identify them in the content, organization, or delivery.

Third, practice outloud. Yes, we know that no speaker enjoys listening to himself, but this is the best method for preparing for your delivery. You can present outloud to yourself in a mirror or give it to a mentor who will give you honest feedback. Make the best use of technology, and record yourself with an audio or video recorder. This is the best way to evaluate your own speaking. It is always better to identify mistakes during the preparation stages rather than during the speech itself. Humility here and in other aspects of your life provides excellent teaching moments: We cannot grow as speakers if our weaknesses are not brought to our attention. There is no substitute for guided preparation. The more, the better.

15

POWERPOINT ETIQUETTE

While preachers have used visual aids for thousands of years (e.g., consider Ezekiel for an exemplar), twenty-first century speakers must consider how to use presentation aids like PowerPoint effectively. Although audiences have come to expect PowerPoint from preachers, we have found that far too many speakers use it ineffectively, with the slides often detracting from the verbal message. Below we offer recommendations for PowerPoint use within sermons.

The Purpose of PowerPoint

Much like nonverbal communication (see chapter 13), PowerPoint should complement and regulate your verbal message. Your PowerPoint should not repeat or substitute your message. Moreover, a PowerPoint should not take the place of the sermon; the spoken word must remain central in a sermon. Some preachers put nearly every word they say on the PowerPoint, but such heavy use detracts from the power of the spoken word. Others read directly from the PowerPoint. Such sloppy presentation puts the PowerPoint, not the spoken word, as central to the message. Rather, effective speakers complement their spoken word through the PowerPoint, using it to highlight and emphasize important points. Furthermore, it can regulate your message by demonstrating transitions between major and minor points. When used correctly, PowerPoint offers your audience a better understanding of your spoken word.

For Beginning Speakers

Just as beginning drivers practice in empty parking lots rather than busy highways, beginning speakers should aim for simplicity. Integrating PowerPoint into your sermon takes practice and skill. For new speakers, we recommend minimizing or perhaps even avoiding PowerPoint. Become seasoned with the other aspects of speaking before attempting PowerPoint. We have seen too many beginning speakers lose track of their message because of PowerPoint issues to recommend its use early in your speaking life. As a further recommendation, you can also have one slide with the lesson title on the screen while you speak or a handful of slides with titles of your major points. Such use satisfies the audience's expectation of PowerPoint while allowing you to focus on your message. Likewise, when you begin to introduce PowerPoint to your lessons, begin simple before trying anything complex. It is wise to walk before running with PowerPoint.

Content Features

When constructing your PowerPoint, you first must decide what to include on the slides. While your decision may depend on your audience, your speaking style, your comfort with PowerPoint, your organizational pattern, and your topic, we will offer two general recommendations. First, include only materials that complement your spoken word. If you think that something will detract from the message, do not include it. Second, simple is best. Your goal is not to impress your audience but to increase their understanding of the Scripture. Simplicity will accomplish this goal.[30]

When formatting your slides, begin with the heading. Rather than putting a phrase or headline at the top of the slide, use a declarative sentence or question. This will focus your content on the slide. As an example, if you are preaching a sermon on grace, one point may concern God's gracious nature. Rather than putting "God's Grace" at the top, writing "God has been gracious to his people." would be more effective. Your following content can then expound on this point.

After creating an impactful heading, you must decide what to include on the rest of the slide. You have options: Bible passages, summaries of main points, key words, definitions, pictures, charts, etc. Whatever content you include, ensure that it is complementary to the spoken word and simple. All slides should not have an identical format; rather, vary your slide by what will supplement your message. For example, if you are preaching on Jesus' prayer in Gethsemane, you may include a picture of the garden itself, an important verse from the narrative, a key point about prayer, or a chart summarizing the main stages of the story.

We have a few other recommendations about content. First, have a backup plan. Murphy's law applies most fully to church PowerPoint, so always be prepared for your presentation not to work. Have a hard copy of your lesson ready, and be able to speak without the PowerPoint. Second, avoid passing out copies of the PowerPoint before the presentation. Doing so decreases your audience's attention as they feel as though they already have the information. Finally, avoid bullet points unless offering a list. Be more thoughtful with your PowerPoint, crafting better content on your slide.

Design Features

Having decided what to include on the slides, you must now give thought to how to design the slides. Again, simplicity is critical. When including text, follow the 6x6 rule: Include no more than six words across by six lines down on a slide.[31] Including more than this number overwhelms an audience. Also, consider what font to use, whether serif or sans serif. Avoid fonts that are difficult to read, and choose one that matches the tone of your presentation. Likewise, consider what font size to use; this will depend on the size of the auditorium and the size of the screen. Ask other speakers what size they have found easy to read, or test it yourself. Remember that many older members have difficulty with vision, so bigger is better with fonts.

In conjunction with the font, also consider how to format the slides themselves. Color is an important factor. Light text on a dark background often shows up best, but this may depend on the lighting of the auditorium and the power of the projector. When choosing colors, avoid ones that are difficult to read or distracting. Choose two or three theme colors, and stick with those for the PowerPoint. Also, avoid special effects. Animations can help you transition between slides, but make sure they do not distract from the presentation. Finally, consider what software will best meet your needs. Microsoft PowerPoint is the most popular software, but you can also use alternatives like Google Slides or Prezi.

On the Inclusion of Scripture

A special consideration preachers must make when using PowerPoint is how many Bible passages to include on the PowerPoint itself. While some preachers prefer their audiences to read from their personal Bibles and do not include any passages on the slides, others put every passage they read on the PowerPoint. The ideal solution is somewhere in between. Include passages that are critical to your message. Doing so keeps your audience's attention on the written Word and your spoken words while also highlighting key passages. You may also choose to underline key phrases for special emphasis.

SECTION FIVE

Conclusion

16

CONCLUSION

Reflecting on Your Message

The end of your talk is just the beginning of your journey to preaching the gospel of Christ. In your speaking, we urge you to have the mindset of Paul, who admonished the Thessalonians to "excel still more" (1 Thes 4.10). Further strengthen your abilities, and correct your weaknesses. The precious nature of the gospel demands our best efforts, and we should never cease in our quest to improve our presentational skills of it.

Practically, we recommend two sources for finding recommendations for improvement. First, seek the feedback of church leaders you respect. Brethren will generally encourage you after your talk. Thank them for their words, but do not allow such edification to puff up your ego. Remember that all that we say should be to the "glory of God" (1 Pet 4.11), not our own glory. After your talk, solicit the feedback of specific brethren who will give you honest feedback for improvement. Perhaps even ask to sit down with an elder or evangelist who heard your talk, and ask them for specific recommendations for improvement. Just as Paul taught Timothy, you can learn from the wisdom of experienced speakers.

Second, watch or listen to your talk. As we have admitted before, listening to yourself can be awkward, but it is the best avenue for identifying your strengths and weaknesses as a speaker. As you watch or listen, make notes of what you did well and what improvements you need to make, and then go about practicing to improve. If you recognize that you spoke too fast, practice slowing down. If you recognize that you made a weird gesture, work on using your hands more effectively. If you recognize that the body of your speech did not flow well, work on your organization. Again, always seek to "excel still more." God is worthy of our best efforts.

Putting It All Together

Like learning any new skill, public speaking requires devotion and work. We know that many aspects of public speaking can intimidate the novice speaker, but following the principles we have offered in this book will start you on a journey to success. Remember, good speaking has three important facets, COD: content, organization, and delivery. Taken together, COD (well-reasoned content, a fluid organization, and a clear delivery) provide a synergistic formula for an effective speech. May God bless you as you work to become an effective messenger of His Word, and may you bless God always in your presentation of His holy gospel.

APPENDICES

APPENDIX A

Audience Analysis Form

Demographic factors that will assist in choosing a topic:
- How many will be present?
- What is the age range?
- What is the gender mix?
- What is the educational range?
- What professions are represented?
- What is the prior knowledge of the audience?
- What is the level of spiritual maturity of the audience?

Psychographic and contextual factors that will assist in deciding how to present the topic:
- Is the chosen topic appropriate for this audience and occasion?
- What is my ethos (reputation) with this audience and this topic?
- What are the relevant values that my audience hold dear?
- What is their general attitude toward this topic?

- What are their relevant beliefs toward this topic?
- Will my audience be able to retain the presented information in this amount of time?

Appendix B
Sample Sermon Outline
Title: Coming to Know God

I. Introduction

> Notice that the outline is extemporaneous.

   A. The age of social media has changed the way that we form relationships.

> Remember to write nonverbal reminders (e.g., slow down).

      1. I am still young enough to remember the days before Facebook, when the way to make friends was dominantly face-to-face.

> The intro. uses a story from Facebook.

      2. However, now we can make "friends" by the click of a button.

      3. Whether our Facebook "friends" count as real friends is a discussion for another day, but it does highlight an important relational question: how do we come to *know* someone else?

> Seeking to gain the audience's attention, we offer a rationale for the speech.

         a) We, of course, can learn basic information and interests from social media.

         b) But only through time together and communication can we really come to know someone.

   B. As difficult as it can be in the age of social media to come to know others, we then must consider, how do we come to *know* God?

> Giving thought to audience analysis, this speech could be presented to most audiences.

      1. Making relationships on earth gives life richness.

      2. Yet if we believe there is a God, each of us must ask how we come to know Him and then to pursue that path.

> This is the thesis of the speech, also forecasting main points.

   C. <u>I would like to propose Psalm 103:7 as a model for how we come to know God: we must know His works and His ways.</u>

II. The Works of God
   A. First, let's examine our focus text before we consider further how to come to know God.

> A slide on a visual aid with "Works of God" could be effective.

      1. Psalm 103 provides a psalm of praise to God, emphasizing the lovingkindness of God, so let's read the Scriptures together.
      2. [READ Psalm 103:1-14.]

> Notice that this is a complementary organizational pattern, with two main points.

         a) Let's pay special attention to verse 7: "He made known His ways to Moses and His acts [or works] to the people of Israel."
         b) So if we come to know God, we must know both His works and His ways.

   B. Let's first consider what it means to know the works of God.

> The Exodus provides supporting material.

      1. In the context of Psalm 103, David praises God for what He has done, drawing upon God's actions among the generation of Israelites who came out of Egypt.

> Using all caps ensures you do not skip the reading.

         a) [READ Exodus 34:10.]
         b) Indeed, God did marvelous works among that generation.
            (1) [READ Psalm 78:11-16, 42-55.]
            (2) God did great natural wonders and demonstrated His power through what He did.

> Notice how this speech discusses a topic—knowing God—in light of a text, Psalm 103.

            (3) Through the sending of plagues, the parting of the Red Sea, the miraculous giving of water, and the performing of other acts, God demonstrated great works.

> If you would like a stronger PowerPoint, use a picture of the Exodus with this claim on a slide.

         c) So then, knowing the works of God means that we know what God has done.

2. As David remembered God's works in Psalm 103, we likewise should learn and know God's works.

> Parallelism adds vivid language.

   a) We should know that He made the world.
   b) We should know that He brought Israel from Egyptian bondage.

> Think how your vocalics should complement your words in this section.

   c) We should know that He gave Israel the land by the might of His hand.
   d) We should know that He performed miracles in Israel's presence.
   e) And we should know that He sent His Son to die on the cross.

3. Only when we know what God has done (i.e., His works!) will we begin to come to know Him.

III. The Ways of God

   A. While our knowledge of God should begin with learning His works, it should lead to learning His ways.

> This summary aids comprehension.

   1. Indeed, Israel's knowledge of God's works was not enough to keep them in the way of righteousness.
   2. [READ Psalm 78:32.]

   B. Psalm 103:7 shows us that God "made known His ways to Moses," so we should look to Moses' life for a more complete knowledge of God.

   1. Moses knew God's ways.
      a) [READ Exodus 33:12-23.]

> Notice how the life of Moses warrants this claim (i.e., Toulmin model).

      b) In this incredible interaction, Moses was presented with God's glory (i.e., His graciousness and lovingkindness).
      c) So then while knowing God's works means that we know what He has done, knowing God's ways means that we know who He is.

   2. David likewise knew God's ways.

> **The second passage offers further evidence.**

a) [READ Psalm 103:6-14.]
b) Although David was never presented with God's glory as Moses was, He still came to know who God was by meditating on His character and nature.

> **Psalm 103 adds to the speech's pathos.**

c) David, we see from Psalm 103, saw God as righteous, just, merciful, gracious, slow to anger, abounding in steadfast love, relenting in anger, forgiving, compassionate, and all-knowing.

   3. Only when we learn what God has done and then consider who He is will we learn the ways of God.

IV. Conclusion

  A. So while social media may be changing the way that we come to know other people, the model we use for coming to know God has not changed; we must learn His works and know His ways.

  B. I will close by offering two practical recommendations as we come to know God better.

    1. First, let us continually pursue knowledge of God.

> **Consider how your nonverbal delivery, especially vocalics, should change at this part.**

a) David was a man after God's own heart.
b) Indeed, Psalm 103 shows us that David had a deep, personal knowledge of God, one that increased throughout His life.
c) We should likewise pursue deeper knowledge of God each day, of His works and ways.

    2. Second, let us walk in His way.

a) [READ Psalm 86:8-11.]

> **Repeat for retention.**

b) As we know God's ways, we should walk in His way.

  C. So then, let us know God by learning His works and His ways, and may our ways be like His.

APPENDIX C

Speaking Evaluation Form

Oral Delivery	Vocal quality, pitch, rate, enunciation, pronunciation, grammar, accuracy, sincerity	1	2	3
Nonverbal Communication	Eye contact, facial and body gestures, posture	1	2	3
Content	*Information:* clear, sufficient, relevant, interesting, variety	1	2	3
	Reasoning: sufficient, amount, accurate, clear, applicable	1	2	3
	Emotional Appeals: relevant to attitudes, variety, adequate strength; appropriate to topic, audience, and occasion	1	2	3

Organization: attention-getting introduction, clear key idea, focused on topic, sufficient supporting materials, apparent and appropriate conclusion   1 2 3

Topic: suitable for audience, sufficiently narrowed   1 2 3

COMMENTS:

APPENDIX D

Public Speaking Anxiety (PSA) Evaluation Form

Here is a short test that will give you insight into your anxiety level. Because it comes from a college textbook on public speaking, interpret the questions as they apply to the context of Biblical talks and sermons.

In the blank beside the statement, write the number of the response that best reflect your feelings.

(1) Strongly disagree

(2) Disagree

(3) Agree

(4) Strongly agree

_____ 1. I begin to get nervous the moment the speech is assigned.

_____ 2. I feel panicky because I don't know how to create a speech.

_____ 3. I usually feel nervous the day before I have to speak.

_____ 4. The night before the speech I can't sleep well.

_____ 5. I'm afraid people will think I'm dumb or boring or weird in some way.

_____ 6. On the morning of the speech, I am really tense.

_____ 7. I find it difficult to think positively about giving a speech.

_____ 8. I think my physical reactions are greater than those that other people experience.

_____ 9. During my speech I actually think I'll faint.

_____ 10. I continue to worry even after the speech is over.

Add your scores.

_____ Total score

0–5	You're virtually fearless.
6–15	Your level of anxiety is quite normal.
16–25	Your level of anxiety may give you problems.
26–30	Consider getting some help. Go back and look at the areas that bother you most, then develop specific strategies to help you with your unique stresses.

Taken from *Public Speaking: Concepts and Skills for a Diverse Society, 3rd edition*, Cella Jafee. Used by permission, Wadsworth, Thomson Learning.

APPENDIX E

Recommended Resources for Speech

Speech Resources

Dan O'Hair, Rob Stewart, and Hannah Rubenstein, *A Speaker's Guidebook: Text and Reference*, 6th ed. (Boston: Bedford St. Martin's, 2015). This is perhaps the most extensive and readable introductory guide to public speaking.

John A. Broadus, *On the Preparation and Delivery of Sermons*, 4th ed. (New York: HarperCollins, 1979). This classic text on homiletics focuses especially on sermons.

Online Resources

www.afirstlook.com. This website overviews most of the communication theories that we discussed in this book and will help you think about communication more critically.

www.coursera.org/specializations/public-speaking. If you are not able to take a collegiate public speaking course, this is a great option, offering four courses on the subject.

www.americanrhetoric.com. This website indexes many exemplar rhetorical speeches.

www.ted.com. TED has popularized speech in our culture; you can learn from great speakers about how to improve your own speaking.

livestream.com/wearefc/2018–2019. Florida College posts its daily chapel services, which includes a daily devotional. Listening to seasoned preachers in chapel and on other websites can improve your speaking.

www.toastmasters.org. Joining a group like Toastmasters gives you a chance to practice your skills.

Notes

1. All Bible passages are from the English Standard Version, 2011.

2. See Book XII of Quintilian's *Intitutio Oratoria*.

3. This quotation is usually attributed to Thomas Paine.

4. For more on the importance of character in preaching, see Dee Bowman *Common Sense Preaching* (Temple Terrace: Florida College Press, 1999).

5. William J. McGuire, "Personality and Attitude Change: An Information-Processing Theory," in *Psychological Foundations of Attitudes*, ed. A. Greenwald, T. Brock, and T. Ostrom. (New York: Academic Press, 1968).

6. Andrew D. Wolvin and Carolyn Gwyn Coakley, *Listening* (Dubuque, Iowa: Brown, 1996).

7. Judi Brownwell, *Listening: Attitudes, Principles, and Skills*, 3rd ed. (Boston: Allyn & Bacon, 2006), p. 9.

8. Brant R. Burleson, "The Constructivist Approach to Person-Centered Communication: Analysis of a Research Exemplar," in *Rethinking Communication: Paradigm Exemplars*, ed. Brenda Dervin, Lawrence Grossberg, Barbara J. O'Keefe, and Ellen Wartella (Newbury Park, CA: Sage, 1989), pp. 29-46.

9. Gerald R. Miller and Mark Steinberg, *Between People: A New Analysis of Interpersonal Communication* (Chicago: Science Research Associates, 1975).

10. Martin Fishbein, "A Behavior Theory Approach to the Relations Between Beliefs About an Object and the Attitude Toward the Object," in *Readings in Attitude Theory and Measurement*. (New York: Wiley, 1967).

11. Barbara J. O'Keefe, "The Logic of Message Design: Individual Differences in Reasoning About Communication," *Communication Monographs* 55 (1988): 80-103.

12. Muzafer Sherif, Carolyn Sherif, and Roger Nebergall, *Attitude and Attitude Change: The Social Judgment-Involvement Approach* (Philadelphia: Saunders, 1965).

13. Martin J. Eppler and Jeanne Mengis, "The Concept of Information Overload: A Review of Literature From Organization Science, Accounting, Marketing, MIS, And Related Disciplines," *The Information Society 20* (2004): 325-344.

14. Stephen R. Toulmin, Richard D. Rieke, and Allan Janik. *An Introduction to Reasoning* (New York: Macmillan, 1984).

15. Aristotle, *Rhetoric*, trans. W. Rhys Roberts (New York: Modern Library, 1954).

16. Mortimer J. Adler, *How to Speak, How to Listen* (New York: Simon & Schuster, 1983).

17. Dan O'Hair, Rob Stewart, and Hannah Rubenstein, *A Speaker's Guidebook: Text and Reference*, 6th ed. (Boston: Bedford St. Martin's, 2015).

18. Walter R. Fisher, *Human Communication as Narration: Toward a Philosophy of Reason, Value, and Action*. (Columbia, SC: University of South Carolina, 1987).

19. Graham D. Bodie, "A Racing Heart, Rattling Knees, and Ruminative Thoughts: Defining, Explaining, and Treating Public Speaking Anxiety," *Communication Education 59* (2010): 70-105.

20. Andrew J. Elliot and Marcy A. Church, "A Hierarchical Model of Approach and Avoidance Achievement Motivation," *Journal of Personality and Social Psychology, 72* (1997).

21. Joint Congressional Committee on Inaugural Ceremonies, "The 37th Presidential Inauguration," Senate.gov, accessed August 22, 2018, https://www.inaugural.senate.gov/about/past-inaugural-ceremonies/37th-inaugural-ceremonies/.

22. Signmund Freud, "Instincts And Their Vicissitudes," in *The Standard Edition of the Complete Works of Sigmund Freud*, ed. and trans. J. Strachey (London: Hogarth Press, 1915), vol. 14, pp. 111-142.

23. Renee Edwards, James M. Honeycutt, and Kenneth S. Zagacki, "Imagined Interaction as an Element of Social Cognition," *Western Journal of Communication, 52,* (1998), 23-45.

24. William Strunk & Elwyn B. White, *The Elements of Style*, 4th ed. (Boston: Allyn & Bacon, 1999).

25. Founders Online, "Thomas Jefferson to John Minor, 30 August 1814, including Thomas Jefferson to Bernard Moore, [ca. 1773?]," Nationalarchives.gov, accessed August 22, 2018, https://founders.archives.gov/documents/Jefferson/03-07-02-0455.

26. Albert Mehrabian, *Nonverbal Communication* (Chicago:Aldine-Atherton, 1972).

27. Mark L. Knapp and Judith A. Hall, *Nonverbal Communication in Human Interaction,* 7th ed. (Boston: Wadsworth, 2010).

28. Judee K. Burgoon, Laura K. Guerrero, and Kory Floyd, *Nonverbal Communication* (New York: Pearson, 2016).

29. David B. Buller and R. Kelly Aune, "The Effects of Vocalics and Nonverbal Sensitivity on Compliance: A Speech Accommodation Theory Explanation," *Human Communication Research, 14* (1988).

30. Jean-Luc Doumont, "The Cognitive Style of PowerPoint: Slides Are Not All Evil," *Technical Communication, 52* (2004), pp. 64-70.

31. Edward R. Tufte. *The Cognitive Style of PowerPoint: Pitching Out Corrupts Within* (Cheshire, CT: Graphics Press, 2006).

*For a full listing of DeWard Publishing
Company books, visit our website:*

www.deward.com

www.ingramcontent.com/pod-product-compliance
Lightning Source LLC
Chambersburg PA
CBHW031451040426
42444CB00007B/1053